FEMALE SUICIDE BOMBERS

June 2004

*****

The views expressed in this report are those of the author and do not necessarily reflect the official policy or position of the Department of the Army, the Department of Defense, or the U.S. Government. This report is cleared for public release; distribution is unlimited.

*****

My thanks to Colonel Russ Santala for suggesting this truly interesting topic. Thanks also go to Colonel Harry Tomlin for helping me think through the tough questions. Additionally, the U.S. Army War College Library staff is absolutely excellent. This paper would not have been so well researched without the help of the entire staff, but most especially Mr. Bohdan I. Kohutiak and Ms. Jane E. Gibish, who vigilantly watched for information on female suicide bombers. My appreciation also to Mr. Shawn Mosholder, the Strategic Research Program (SRP) template wizard, for his assistance in final preparation and formatting. My final thanks to Dr. Anna Waggener who was the absolute best SRP advisor—kept me on track and focused on strategic issues with encouragement, help, advice, and good will.

*****

*****

*****

The Strategic Studies Institute publishes a monthly e-mail newsletter to update the national security community on the research of our analysts, recent and forthcoming publications, and upcoming conferences sponsored by the Institute. Each newsletter also provides a strategic commentary by one of our research analysts. If you are interested in receiving this newsletter, please let us know by e-mail at *SSI_Newsletter@carlisle.army.mil* or by calling (717) 245-3133.

PREFACE

The U.S. Army War College provides an excellent environment for selected military officers and government civilians to reflect and use their career experience to explore a wide range of strategic issues. To assure that the research developed by Army War College students is available to Army and Department of Defense leaders, the Strategic Studies Institute publishes selected papers in its Carlisle Papers in Security Strategy Series.

Ms. Debra Zedalis, member of the Army War College Class of 2004, is the author of this paper. She reviews the history of female suicide bombers, focuses on their characteristics, analyzes recent changes in their use by various terrorist organizations, and provides implications of change within a strategic assessment of future female suicide bombings.

ANTULIO J. ECHEVARRIA II
Director of Research
Strategic Studies Institute

iii

ABOUT THE AUTHOR

DEBRA D. ZEDALIS is a Department of the Army civilian who was a member of the U.S. Army War College Class of 2004. Prior to attending the Army War College, Ms. Zedalis was the Chief of Staff for the Installation Management Agency, Europe Region, Heidelberg, Germany. She has worked for the U.S. Army in Europe since 1988, serving as the Chief of the Management Division, Office of the Deputy Chief of Staff for Resource Management, as well as the Chief of the Installation Management Support Division, Office of the Deputy Chief of Staff for Personnel and Installation Management. Prior to her European assignment, Ms. Zedalis worked at the U.S. Army Armor Center and Fort Knox as a program analyst and manpower analyst. She holds a Master's Degree in Business Administration from Syracuse University and a Bachelor of Arts in Managerial Psychology from the University of Kentucky.

ABSTRACT

Suicide bombers are today's weapon of choice. Terrorists are using suicide bombers because they are a low cost, low technology, and low risk weapon. Suicide bombers are readily available, require little training, leave no trace behind, and strike fear into the general population. The success of suicide bombers depends upon an element of surprise, as well as accessibility to targeted areas or populations. Both of these required elements have been enjoyed by women suicide bombers. Female suicide bombers were used in the past; however, the recent spate of them in different venues, in different countries, and for different terrorist organizations forces us to study this terrorist method.

This research paper reviews historical female suicide bombers, focuses on female suicide bomber characteristics, analyzes recent changes in application by various terrorist organizations, and provides implications of change within a strategic assessment of future female suicide bombings.

FEMALE SUICIDE BOMBERS

I have to tell the world that if they do not defend us, then we have to defend ourselves with the only thing we have, our bodies. Our bodies are the only fighting means at our disposal.

Hiba, 28-year old, mother of five,
Suicide Bomber Trainee

Suicide bombers are today's weapon of choice. An action that was once so surprising, horrific, and terrifying has now become the daily fare of the nightly news. "From Jerusalem to Jakarta and from Bali to Baghdad, the suicide bomber is clearly the weapon of choice for international terrorists."[1] The raw number of suicide attacks is climbing;[2] suicide bombs are now used by 17 terror organizations in 14 countries.[3] "In terms of casualties, suicide attacks are the most efficient form of terrorism. From 1980 to 2001, suicide attacks accounted for 3 percent of terrorist incidents but caused half of the total deaths due to terrorism—even if one excludes the unusually large number of fatalities of 9/11."[4] Into this boiling cauldron of terror, a new element has been added—women as suicide bombers. The success of suicide bombers considerably depends upon surprise and accessibility to targets. Both of these requirements have been met by using women. The recent spate of female suicide bombers in different venues, different countries, and different terrorist organizations warrants careful study of this strategic weapon.

Prior to September 11, 2001, the use of suicide bombers was not seen by the U.S. public as a major threat; however, this weapon now evokes a visceral response. The Department of Homeland Security (DHS) Alert 03-025 provided warnings of male and female suicide bombers,[5] and New York City was on heightened alert in December 2003 over fears of an attack by a female suicide bomber.[6] Jessica Stern, a terrorism expert, recently criticized DHS procedures and warned of the dangers of ignoring female terrorists: "The official profile of a typical terrorist—developed by the DHS to scrutinize visa applicants and resident aliens—applies only to men. Under a program put in place after September 11, 2001, males aged between 16-45 are subject to special scrutiny; women are not."[7] Terrorists seek out vulnerabilities in the enemy government's countermeasures, so lack of scrutiny of women entering the United States could encourage Al Qaeda to use them.[8]

This paper reviews the history of female suicide bombers, focuses on bomber characteristics, analyzes recent attacks, and predicts future trends within a strategic assessment of future female suicide bombings. According to a terrorist expert, "This research is particularly demanding as there are not enough reports with descriptions of the cases, there is not enough documentation on how these women are treated in terrorist groups, there are not enough testimonies, and it is difficult to profile these murderers."[9] Most chilling, however, is that those who could tell us their stories—those who went through with this death act—cannot share their thoughts and motivation.

HISTORY OF SUICIDE BOMBING

"A long view of history reveals that suicide terrorism existed as early as the 11th century. The Assassins (*Ismalis-Nizari*), Muslim fighters, adopted suicide terrorism as a strategy to advance the cause of Islam. These perpetrators perceived their deaths as acts of martyrdom for the glory of God."[10] Further,

The Assassins' aim, like that of Islamist extremists today, was to spread a "pure" version of Islam. Like contemporary suicide bombers, they considered their own lives to be sacrificial offerings. Unlike today's suicide bombers, the Assassins murdered particular individuals rather than randomly targeting people whose only crime is to be in the wrong place at the wrong time.[11]

Female suicide bombers are relatively new. Their first known attack came in 1985 when a 16-year-old girl, Khyadali Sana, drove a truck into an Israeli Defense Force convoy and killed two soldiers. Since then, women have driven bomb-laden vehicles, carried bomber "bags," and strapped massive explosives and metal implements on their bodies in Lebanon, Sri Lanka, Chechnya, Israel, and Turkey. Terrorist groups which have publicized their use of females include the Syrian Socialist National Party (SSNP/PPS), the Liberation Tigers of Tamil Eelam (LTTE), the Kurdistan Workers Party (PKK), Chechen rebels, Al Aqsa Martyrs, Palestinian Islamic Jihad (PIJ), and, most recently, Hamas.

There are many "firsts" in this listing of organized feminine terror. While the SSNP has the distinction of deploying the first female suicide bomber, the "LTTE became the world's foremost suicide bombers and proved the tactic to be so unnerving and effective that their methods and killing innovations were studied and copied, most notably in the Middle East."[12] The LTTE has committed the most attacks, close to 200, using women bombers in 30-40 percent. The largest number killed (170) was in Moscow in October 2002 when Chechen rebels (including a high percentage of women) held hostages in the Theater Center, and the police killed 129 captives and 41 rebels in a futile rescue effort. During the last 2 years, Palestinian suicide bombers have carried out the largest number of attacks.

Not all bombers are known nor are all the data known to be correct. The youngest appears to be either Khyadali Sana (SSNP/PPS, 1985), 16, or Laila Kaplan, (PKK, 1996), 17; the oldest was Shagir Karima Mahmud (SSNP/PPS, 1987), 37. The first LTTE bomber, Dhanu, successfully killed Prime Minister Rajiv Gandhi in May 1991. The first female PKK suicide bombing (June 1996), which may also be the first instance of an apparently pregnant bomber, killed six Turkish soldiers; the bomber's name is unknown. The first Russian "Black Widow" or *saliheen*, Hawa Barayev, acted on behalf of the Chechen rebels in June 2000 and killed 27 Russian Special Forces soldiers. In January 2002, the first *istish-hadiyat* (female martyr) in Israel, representing the Al Aqsa Martyrs' Brigade, was Wafa Idris, a paramedic who detonated a 22-pound body bomb filled with nails and metal objects in a shopping district. Wafa killed an 81-year-old man and injured more than 100. The first PIJ bomber was a 19-year-old student, Hiba Daraghmeh, who detonated a bomb in a shopping mall, killing three people. The second PIJ bomber, 29-year-old lawyer Hanadi Jaradat, also received much publicity as she strolled into a highly frequented restaurant in October 2003 and killed 21 Israeli and Arab men, women, and children. The most recent "first" was the first female Hamas bomber, 22-year-old Reem al-Reyashi, who, on January 14, 2004, killed four Israeli soldiers at a checkpoint. Of particular note is that Reem was also a mother who left behind a husband, a 3-year-old son, and a 1-year-old daughter. A "first" yet to strike is the first female suicide bomber representing Al Qaeda (See Tables 1 and 2. Table 1 lists successful female suicide bombers. Table 2 shows those who were unsuccessful for some reason or who are trainees.)

SUICIDE BOMBERS

A suicide bomber, someone willing to die for a cause, is puzzling. What is a suicide bomber? Why use suicide bombers? Who becomes a suicide bomber? Most importantly, why would one voluntarily die in order to kill other innocent people?

What is a Suicide Bomber?

The Institute for Counter-Terrorism (ICT) defined suicide bombing as an "operational method in which the very act of the attack is dependent upon the death of the perpetrator. The terrorist is fully aware that if she/he does not kill her/himself, the planned attack will not be implemented."[13] "Suicide bomber" is an emotionally-laden term. Some describe these individuals as "homicide bombers" or "suicide terrorists" to emphasize the murder and terror brought about by this act; others deem these individuals as "martyrs" who have died for their faith.

NAME	DATE	WHERE OCCURRED	AGE	STATUS	ORGANIZATION	KILLED	WOUNDED	NOTES
Andaleeb Takafka	12-Apr-02	Israel	20	Seam-stress	Al Aqsa Martyrs Bde	6	104	Fourth female suicide bomber. Detonated bag full of explosives at a bus stop. From Bethlehem.
Aayat al-Akhras	29-Mar-02	Israel	18		Al Aqsa Martyrs Bde	2	25	Killed 2 in Jerusalem supermarket. Taped a martyr statement. Engaged. Came from Dehaisa Refugee Camp near Bethlehem. Cousins killed/wounded. Third female suicide bomber in Israel. Recently saw neighbor killed in his home while playing with his child.
Dareen Abu Aysheh	27-Feb-02	Israel	21	Suspect	Al Aqsa Martyrs Bde	0	4	Blew herself up at roadblock. Student at Al-Najah University. Came from village on West Bank. Went to Hamas to volunteer but they turned her down. Single, religious. Second female suicide bomber in Israel. Vowed revenge for Israeli troops shooting pregnant women at checkpoints. Cousin killed himself 1 month earlier.
Wafa Idris	27-Jan-02	Israel	28	Para-medic	Al Aqsa Martyrs Bde	1	>100	First female suicide bomber in Israel. Detonated bomb in shopping district. Divorced, no children. Lived in Amari Refugee Camp. 22 to bomb with nails and metal objects. 3 brothers in Fatah. Treated wounded, hit 3 times by Israeli rubber bullets.
Hawa Barayev	6-Jun-00	Chechnya			Chechens	27	0	Drove into building housing Russian Special Forces. Man accompanied her. First "black widow"
Zulikhan Elikhadzhiyeva	5-Jul-03	Russia	20		Chechens	15	60	2 female suicide bombers at Moscow Rock Concert. Zulikhan was from Chechen village. Brother is Wahhabe leader. Family home not destroyed, no close relatives killed. Some say brother kidnapped her.
Unknown	5-Jun-03	Russia			Chechens	17	15	Flagged down bus carrying military personnel to the air base. Third attack by female in 3 weeks. Officials believe rebels influenced by Islamic militants.
Unknown	14-May-03	Russia			Chechens	18	2	2 bombers. Religious Festival. Tried to assassinate Russian leader Akmud Kadyrov. Killed bodyguard.
Unknown	1-May-03	Russia			Chechens	59	1	1 woman and 2 men carried out truck bomb suicide attack. Attack at Govt complex in Nother Chechnya.

Table 1. Successful Suicide Bombers.

NAME	DATE	WHERE OCCURRED	AGE	STATUS	ORGANIZATION	KILLED	WOUNDED	NOTES
Unknown	1-May-03	Russia			Chechens	59		1 woman and 2 men carried out truck bomb suicide attack. Attack at Govt complex in Norther Chechnya.
Reem al-Reyashi	14-Jan-04	Israel	22		Hamas and Al Aqsa Martyrs Bde	4	7	First Hamas suicide bomber, first mother in Israel. Requested medical help, blew up at inspection checkpt. Made video (anti-Zionist). Left behind 3-year-old son and 1 year-old daughter. 10 lb bomb w/ball bearings and screws. Came from middle-class family in Gaza City. Husband had no knowledge of her plans. Al Aqsa also claimed
Unknown	Dec-99	Sri Lanka			Liberation Tigers of Tamil Eelam (LTTE)			Attempted to assassinate Sri Lanka President Chandrika Kumaratunga
Dhanu	20-May-91	Sri Lanka			LTTE			Killed Prime Minister Rajiv Gandhi
Hanadi Jaradat	4-Oct-03	Israel	29	Lawyer	Palestinian Islamic Jihad (PIJ)	21	>12	At Maxim's Restaurant.
Hiba Daraghmeh	1-May-03	Israel	19	Student	PIJ	3		First Islamic Jihad. Fifth female. Attack in mall.
Ozen Fatma	17-Nov-99	Turkey			Kurdistan Workers Party (PKK)	0	6	Bomb strapped to body, missed target of military convoy.
Gittas Gular	29-Oct-96	Turkey	29		PKK	2	1	Killed policeman. Dressed as pregnant woman, accompanied by another group member. Third bombing by PKK females appearing to be pregnant. Ocalan had urged his troops to imitate Hamas by becoming human bombs.
Leila Kaplan	25-Oct-96	Turkey	17		PKK	5	12	Attacked police headquarters as pregnant woman.
Unknown	30-Jun-99	Turkey			PKK	6	30	First female PKK bomber. Turkish soldiers killed. Bomb strapped to her stomach as if she were pregnant
Shagir Karim a Mahmud	14-Nov-87	Lebanon	37		Syrian Socialist National Party (SSNP/PPS)	7	20	Carried explosive charge hidden in bag into hospital

Table 1. Successful Suicide Bombers (continued).

NAME	DATE	WHERE OCCURRED	AGE	STATUS	ORGANIZATION	KILLED	WOUNDED	NOTES
Sahyoun Soraya	11-Nov-87	Lebanon	20		SSNP,PPS	8	73	Carried suitcase with explosives into airport. Case exploded by remote control
Al Taher Hamidah	28-Nov-85	Lebanon	17		SSNP,PPS			Drove car into SLA checkpoint. 100 Kg of explosives
Khaleralin Miriam	11-Sep-85	Lebanon	18		SSNP,PPS	0	2	Attacked SLA checkpoint
Norma Abu Hassan	17-Jul-85	Lebanon	26		SSNP,PPS	0	?	Targeted Lebanese agents. Blew herself up when she saw soldiers searching for her
Kharib Ibtisam	9-Jul-85	Lebanon	28		SSNP,PPS	0	2 to 6	Attacked SLA post. Left videotape "to kill as many Jews and their assistants as she could"
Khyadali Sana	9-Apr-85	Lebanon	16		SSNP,PPS	2	2	Drove car into IDF convoy. Soldiers killed/injured. Reason given "avenge the oppressive enemy"
Luisa Gazueva	29-Nov-01	Chechnya	Late 20s			2	2	Attempted to kill Cdr Gadzhiev Gadzhiev. Young widow. Rebels did not claim the attack
Unknown	9-Dec-03	Russia				6	14	Outside the National Hotel in Moscow. Belt packed with 2.5 kg of plastic explosives and ball bearings - similar to belt from rock concert although detonating device was of lower quality
Unknown	1-Oct-02	Russia				170	170	Theater Center. 129 captives and 41 rebels killed.
Rusan Tabanci	5-Jul-99	Turkey	19			0	17	Flashed "V" for victory and detonated bomb on body
Esma Yurdakul	27-Mar-99	Turkey	21			0	10	
Unknown	4-Mar-99	Turkey				0	4	In city square. Bomb may have gone off prematurely as suspected target was police station.
Unknown	24-Dec-98	Turkey				1	22	Outside Army barracks; killed herself and passerby
Unknown	1-Dec-98	Turkey				0	14	Kurdish woman outside supermarket frequented by Turkish soldiers

Successful female suicide bombers arrayed alphabetically by organization, country, where bomb attack occurred, and date

Table 1. Successful Suicide Bombers (concluded).

NAME	DATE	WHERE ATTEMPTED	AGE	STATUS	ORGANIZATION	NOTES
Tawfiya Hamamra	May-02	Israel	26	Dreamaker	Al Aqta Martyrs Bde	From village near Jenin in the West Bank. Said reasons for attack were personal, not political. Received 2 days of training. Backed out caught by IDF.
Arin Ahmad	Apr-02	Israel	20	Student		From Bethlehem. Volunteered to carry out an attack to avenge the death of her fiance. Supposed to commit bombing during last week of April with 18-year-old Issa Badir (who went through with her mission). Arrested on Jun 02 by the IDF
Shefa'a Aikuda	Apr-02	Israel	26			Divorced with young child. Arrested by IDF on 11 Apr 02
Unknown	13-Jun-02	Israel	15		Tanzim	From Bethlehem. Recruited by Tanzim through her uncle.
Unknown	14-Jun-02	Israel				Israel Security Forces apprehended 2 female would-be suicide bombers.
Umaya Mohammed Darai	27-Jun-02	Israel	26			Arrested on her way to commit suicide bombing in Israel.
Zarima Muzhakayeva	11-Jul-03	Russia	22	Widow	Chechen	1 lb of military-issue explosives in bag. Lost husband in fighting against the Russians. Explosives similar to those at rock concert. Policeman killed in attempting to detonate.
Marela Dudayeva		Russia	17		Chechen	Captured when bomb-laden truck failed to detonate. None of her relatives have died in the war, not religious.
Thawra (Revolution)				Trainee		Would like to assassinate Ariel Sharon.
Nidal (Struggle)				Trainee		
Jihad (Holy War)			30	Trainee		Mother of a 12 year old son.
Basam (Smile)			16	Trainee		Not to be used as a suicide bomber but being trained in light weapons.
Noar (Light)			24	Trainee		Accountant. Saw her sister killed
Um Sakher (the Mother of Rock)				Trainee		
Safar (Palestine)				Trainee		
Tahreeer (Liberation)				Trainee		
Hiba			26	Trainee		Has 5 children. Father died in 1st intifada, husband was killed 3 years ago while she was pregnant. Two of her brothers have also been killed, brother in law in an Israeli prison.
Leila			22	Trainee		Student. Family member lost homes, friends living in tents, 12 brothers and sisters.

Female suicide bombers who backed out before event, were unsuccessful and caught, or are currently in training. Those listed as trainees are identified by code name.

Table 2. Unuccessful Suicide Bombers.

Why Use Suicide Bombers?

Terrorism has been defined as "a synthesis of war and theater."[14] This descriptor aptly applies to female suicide bombings. Suicide bombing is used because:
- It is a simple and low-cost operation (requiring no escape route or rescue mission).
- It increases the likelihood of mass casualties and extensive damage (since the bomber can choose the exact time, location, and circumstances of the attack).
- There is no fear that interrogated terrorists will surrender important information (because their deaths are certain).
- It has an immense impact on the public and the media (because it precipitates an overwhelming sense of helplessness).[15]

Others note that suicide terrorism "inflicts profound fear and anxiety and produces a negative psychological effect on an entire population and not just on the victims of the actual attack."[16] Finally, a "suicide attack attracts wide media coverage and is seen as a newsworthy event."[17] Female suicide bombers (youngest, oldest, mother, Red Cross worker, jilted fiancé, avenger of dead family members) have an added media aspect which encourages terrorists to capitalize on the sensationalism.

Organizations which routinely use suicide bombers "have utilized the notion of martyrdom and self-sacrifice as a means of last resort against their conventionally more powerful enemies."[18] These groups believe that suicide bombs are successful in bringing notice to their plight and contend that suicide bombers are the only effective weapons they have, in contrast to their enemies' much larger wealth, weapons, soldiers, and political means. Abu Shanab, a Hamas leader, stated that "all that is required is a bomb, a detonator, and a moment of courage, and courage is the scarce resource."[19]

Why Use Female Suicide Bombers?

The use of women as suicide bombers poses conflicts with some fundamental religious leaders' beliefs, while serving the tactical need for a stealthier weapon. In January 2002, Sheikh Ahmed Yassin, the spiritual leader of Hamas, "categorically renounced the use of women as suicide bombers."[20] In March 2002 after the second Fatah bombing, he reported that "Hamas was far from enthusiastic about the inclusion of women in warfare, for reasons of modesty."[21] That position dramatically shifted on January 14, 2004, when the first Hamas female suicide bomber struck. Why was she used? Yassin defended this change as a "significant evolution in our fight. The male fighters face many obstacles,"[22] so women can more easily reach the targets. He concluded his statement by noting that "Women are like the reserve army—when there is a necessity, we use them."[23] Terrorist organizations use women as weapons because they provide:
- Tactical advantage: stealthier attack, element of surprise, hesitancy to search women, female stereotype (e.g., nonviolent).
- Increased number of combatants.
- Increased publicity (greater publicity = larger number of recruits).
- Psychological effect.

"It is the ultimate asymmetric weapon," explained Magnus Ranstorp, director of the Center for the Study of Terrorism and Political Violence. "You can assimilate among the people and then attack with an element of surprise that has an incredible and devastating shock value."[24] In the words of a commander in charge of training future suicide bombers, "The body has become our most potent weapon. When we searched for new ways to resist the security complications facing us, we discovered that our women could be an advantage."[25] One trainer even boastfully described them as the new "Palestinian human precision bomb."[26] Those who study Middle East cultures cite another reason: "The use (of female suicide bombers) by Palestinian militant groups is designed to embarrass the Israeli regime and show that things are so desperate that women are fighting instead of men."[27] Suicide bombers provide the low-cost, low-technology, low-risk weapon that maximizes target destruction and instills fear—women are even more effective with their increased accessibility and media shock value.

Who Becomes a Suicide Bomber?

The answer to this question is elusive for both males and females. Some suggest there are definite trends, others dispute that conclusion, and still others maintain that a profile cannot be developed as it is "unlikely that the search would be successful in creating a set of common denominators that could span several continents, time periods, cultures, and political configurations."[28] Some of the factors assessed included age, education, economic status, and socialization toward violence.[29] The only factor that "all the experts seem to agree on is that suicide bombers are primarily young people."[30] Analysts note "The positive attitudes toward political violence—already well entrenched in persons under 17 years of age (14.5 percent)—actually increases in the population up to the age of 24 (14.9 percent) and decreases thereafter (6 percent at 64 years of age)."[31] In addition to age, it appears that education plays a role as "the percentage increases with the level of education: 8.3 percent among those with an elementary school diploma versus 12.8 percent among those with a university degree."[32]

Profiles may be developed for specific sets of suicide bombers. For example, Jessica Stern profiles the typical male Palestinian suicide bomber (young, unmarried, mosque attendee, etc.). Other experts concur, such as Ariel Merari, a leading Israeli authority on suicide terrorism[33] and Boaz Ganor, Executive Director of the ICT.[34] Additionally, most suicide bombers tend to be of average economic status (although a disproportionate number come from refugee camps).[35] Likewise, "as logical as the poverty-breeds-terrorism argument may seem, studies show that suicide attackers are rarely ignorant or impoverished."[36] Two other critical findings reveal that more than half had spent time in Israeli prisons[37] and "had expressed the desire to avenge the death or injury of a relative or a close friend."[38]

Who Becomes a Female Suicide Bomber?

"The reasons for women's participation in deadly attacks vary greatly and it is hard to generalize, for this phenomenon is too recent and the attacks have been too few. Either not enough research has been conducted yet or the sample size is too small to make effective generalizations."[39] Although the data are limited, female suicide bombers, just like male suicide bombers, have one characteristic which typifies all—they are young. The average age varies from 21.5 (Turkey) to 23 (Lebanon), a small differential. Other characteristics do not hold. Some are widows and others have never been married; some are unemployed and others are professionals; some are poor and others are middle class. Most analysts can easily compare the Black Widows in Russia with the Palestinian suicide bombers, since both appear to be serving "struggles of national identity"[40] with religious overtones. Additionally, as is true of the male counterparts, several female suicide bombers have experienced the loss of a close friend or family member. The selection of women for suicide operations and the methods used to persuade them generally are similar to those employed for men. The recruiters take advantage of the candidates' innocence, enthusiasm, personal distress, and thirst for revenge.[41]

Finally, the question of when to recruit comes into play. Some believe that recruiters of female suicide bombers try to "get them while they are young as the LTTE leaders personally brainwashed preadolescent boys and girls, many of them orphans."[42] Russian authorities seem to believe that "you need complete control of all their conditioning, usually from the time they are 11 or 12."[43] At the same time, however, the Russians obviate their own argument by noting that the Chechen insurgency hasn't been going on long enough to "grow" the number of female suicide bombers who have attacked them.[44] Other Russians believe that the female suicide bombers are "sold" to terrorist organizations, drugged to perform such acts, and/or raped and blackmailed if they do not participate. Finally, as one journalist describing the Black Widows concluded, "There are so many theories to explain the women's motivation that it is impossible to sort through them."[45]

Why Become a Suicide Bomber?

There are "religious, nationalistic, economic, social, and personal rewards" for suicide bombers.[46] Researchers believe there are "few differences between a man and a woman carrying out such a mission. It may be a surprise, but motivations are the same: they do believe, they are committed, they are patriotic, and this is combined with a religious duty."[47]

Religious terrorism is a particularly potent form of violence; religion offers the moral justification for committing seemingly immoral acts. Nationalistic fanatics court suicide bombers and use rhetoric to stir up feelings of patriotism, hatred of the enemy, and a profound sense of victimization.[48] Suicide bombers then see their own actions as being driven by a higher order; they believe their sacrifice will provide rewards for them in the afterlife.[49] Devout Muslims believe that, in death, every martyr, male or female, is welcomed by a minimum of 70 apparitions (houri-el-ein) of unnatural beauty who wipe away the martyrs' sins, open the gates of heaven, and provide them with all the pleasures that God has given to mankind.[50]

Beyond religious and patriotic motivations, suicide bombers may receive large sums of money, improve their family's social status, and enhance their reputation. After their death, their families are showered with honor and receive substantial financial rewards.[51] Additionally, suicide bombers expect to be admired and envied by those left behind. Photographs capture them in heroic positions, and these photos will be used as recruitment posters.[52] In fact, a "study of world attitudes by the Pew Research Center showed ever-rising support for 'martyrs,' and recruiters tell researchers that volunteers are beating down the door to join."[53]

Finally, many organizations deliberately are targeting women for strategic purposes because female suicide bombers receive more media attention. Research has shown that "public perceptions of the level of terrorism in the world appear to be determined not by the level of violence, but rather by the quality of the incidents, the location, and the degree of media coverage."[54] So the media provides both an advertising and recruitment tool for terrorist groups. Analysts noted that, when the first Palestinian female bombing occurred, the "news was given great prominence . . . far more than any male suicide bomber would have received. Women who kill or threaten to kill are hot news. It is a reaction that knows no state or religious boundaries."[55] Experts worry that "if this catastrophe leads to more women following suit, this will attract disproportionate publicity."[56] This disproportionate publicity, in turn, may arouse worldwide sympathies for suicide bombers and can also serve as a terrorist recruitment tool.

How are Female Suicide Bombers Trained?

Until recently, very little has been known about the female suicide bombers' training. Indeed, in February 2003 the ICT published an article which stated that Palestinian female bombers were not trained nor prepared psychologically for suicide attacks.[57] However, the most recent information, which came from women who have either backed out or been unsuccessful in bombing attempts, proved that wrong. Russian Security Forces captured at least two potential female suicide bombers, and the Israeli Army is said to have 17-20 in custody.[58]

Russian officials maintain that the female suicide bombers "were trained abroad by Islamic fundamentalists outside of Russia, are paid for abroad, and are organized by the head of the Arab agents of Al Qaeda."[59] All potential bombers "are thoroughly trained by Arab psychologists and demolition experts,"[60] and "clandestine training centers have become a conveyor belt in turning out female cannon fodder."[61] Zarima Muzhikhoyeva, the first live *shakhidka* (martyr), was captured when her purse filled with 1.5 kilograms of military-issue explosives failed to detonate.

Ms. Muzhikhoyeva's husband was killed in the first war in Chechnya when she was pregnant with her daughter. A female friend offered to help her and agreed to pay her debts, give her grandparents money, and provide for her daughter—all that was required in return was that she choose the true road to Allah. She was taken by rebel fighters to the mountains for 1 month. There, she cooked and washed the fighters' clothes, prayed daily, and listened to the atrocities of the Russian troops in Chechnya. When her training was complete, she went to Moscow and was housed with the two young women who later blew themselves up at a rock concert. After her capture, she led police to the house and yard where they found a buried metal container filled with explosive belts.[62] The Russians released little information from her interrogation or from interrogation of another unsuccessful female suicide bomber, Mareta Dudeyeva.

In Israel, 25-year-old Tawriya Hamamra, from the Al Aqsa Martyrs Brigade, discussed the training she received in May 2002 before she decided to abort her mission. Two weeks before her mission, she was sent to Nablus, met by a Fatah official, placed in a student flat, and began training. Four people trained her in two 45-minute sessions on Friday and Saturday. On Saturday she told the trainers that she had changed her mind. Although they were angry, they allowed her to leave. She was arrested the next day in an Israeli raid in the nearby city of Tulkarm.[63]

The most recent and in-depth look at Palestinian training of female suicide bombers was published in December 2003. The reporter met the commander in charge, trainers, and nine future Palestinian female suicide bombers:

> . . . women were handling explosives and familiarizing themselves with Kalashnikov sub-machineguns. Girls are taught to assemble and dismantle their AK-47 assault rifles, and target practice follows—as do hours of theory about the "enemy and its tactics." The details and outcome of each attack are dissected, revised, debated, and discussed. The women spend as much as 6 hours a day familiarizing themselves with explosives. They are introduced to the bomb belts that will rip their flesh, while killing and maiming those around them. Finally, the girls have to practice moving around with the weight of the explosive belts strapped to their bodies. Sometimes the explosives are distributed around the body; some strapped to their legs, others to their backs or abdomens. "It all depends on the build and shape of the woman and how best to strap her without over-bulging parts of her body," a male handler explained.[64]

IMPLICATIONS OF CHANGE

In March 2002, after an 18-year-old female killed two innocent people in a supermarket in Israel, a professor of Middle East Studies commented: "I have a great fear that, if this continues, they will pull in younger and younger women. Once they break the boundaries of what is accepted on a human level, there are no boundaries."[65] For female suicide bombers, there appear to be few boundaries left to cross.

From a strategic perspective, the most significant change has been the clergy's approval of female martyrs. Suicide bombers believe they are martyrs and are told they are the "true defenders of the oppressed and dispossessed."[66] Many experts perceive the problem to be the "blurring of differences and the increased confusion between nationalism and religiosity."[67] Until the Chechen terrorist campaign, "the use of female suicide bombers was a clear indicator of secular terrorism. The growth in the number of Chechen female suicide bombers signaled the beginning of a change in the position of fundamentalist Islamic organizations regarding the involvement of women in suicide attacks."[68]

Some fundamentalist clerics have expressed theological dilemmas in sanctioning suicide bombing,[69] as Islam explicitly forbids suicide (*inithar*). The Koran states: "And do not kill yourself, for God is indeed merciful to you."[70] Others note that the Prophet Mohammed explicitly forbade suicide and decreed, "He who drinks poison and kills himself will carry his poison in his hand and drink it in Hell for ever and ever."[71] Militant religious leaders thus have asserted that these attacks are acts of martyrdom (*istishhad*) as a means of last resort.[72] And while God punishes those who commit suicide, he rewards the martyr. According to the Koran, "Think not of those who are slain in the cause of God as dead. Nay, they are alive in the presence of the Lord and are granted gifts from him."[73]

"According to the level of religiosity, terrorist organizations have different policies concerning women suicide bombers. Saudia Arabia originally refused to legitimize female suicide bombings as martyrdom; however, in August 2001, the High Islamic Council in Saudi Arabia issued a *fatwa* encouraging Palestinian women to become suicide bombers."[74] Lebanese Muslim cleric Sheikh Mohammed Hussein Fadlallah declared, "It is true that Islam has not asked women to carry out jihad (holy war), but it permits them to take part if the necessities dictate that women should carry out regular military operations or suicide operations."[75] The Koran states that jihad can be carried out by women as well as men, but "most contend that women can serve as combatants only after the male ranks have been depleted. This is the demarcation that had kept Hamas from recruiting women."[76] In January 2004, that demarcation disappeared.

Another strategic concern is the possibility that female suicide bombing is being supported, financed, and directed by a global terror network. Some believe that the "resort to martyrdom can be explained by an increasing level of internationalization between groups in terms of contact, similarity of causes, and examples of strategies."[77] In the Chechen terrorist campaign, "while the groups involved act in the name of an ethnic-nationalist ideology, they are thought to be cooperating with global jihad organizations connected to Al Qaeda and count several 'Afghan alumni' among their commanders."[78] Additionally, in March 2003, "the Saudi-owned *Asharq Al-Awsat* published an e-mail interview with a leader of the female mujahedeen of Al Qaeda. She told them her instructions came from Al Qaeda and the Taliban, mainly via internet."[79] The woman went on to state that the organization was planning "a new attack which would make the United States forget September 11, and that the idea came from the martyr operations carried out by the Palestinian women."[80] She further outlined training methods and potential locations. This communiqué is especially interesting because currently Al Qaeda has

> . . . refrained from including women in their operations except in supporting roles. The religious and ideological leap required [to use female suicide bombers] apparently represents a daunting challenge for Al Qaeda. But if the outcome seems worthwhile, there is a real prospect that Al Qaeda, too, will cross the Rubicon, and then find some religious justification for it.[81]

STRATEGIC ASSESSMENT

"Although profiling suicide bombers may be a fascinating academic challenge, it is less relevant in the real-world struggle against terrorism than understanding the modus operandi of terrorist leaders."[82] Some analysts are concerned most with structural issues: "The most important factor is the organization: almost nobody does this as an individual."[83] They point out the need to counter terrorist organizations: "Since suicide terrorism is an organizational phenomenon, the struggle against it cannot be conducted on an individual level."[84] Most important, "organizations only implement suicide terrorism if their community approves of its use."[85] These organizations, however, are not equally reliant on suicide bombers: "A careful study of all the organizations that have resorted to terrorism since 1983 suggested that the most meaningful distinction among them involves the degree to which suicide bombing is institutionalized."[86] Brian Jenkins, a terrorism expert, agrees. "I think we'd all agree that suicide bombing is abnormal. The fact that abnormal behavior is applauded in the community reflects abnormal conditions. If normal conditions are restored, then normal behavior should return—at least they would be less tolerant of abnormal behavior."[87]

But why would a community view suicide bombing as normal behavior? Some blame military occupation and/or deplorable economic and social conditions.[88] While those may be valid considerations, why haven't all cultures that have endured similar experiences supported suicide bombers? Brian Barber, a psychologist, interviewed 900 young adults from Gaza and a comparison group of Bosnian Muslims "who had also suffered through violence but had not become a source of suicide bombers. Faith was the largest difference: the Palestinians routinely invoked religion to invest personal trauma with social meaning, whereas Bosnians did not consider religion significant to their lives."[89] This is a critical distinction: "The strictly hierarchical nature of religious terrorist groups with a highly disciplined structure and obedient cadre means not only that the main clerical leaders command full control over the political as well as military activities of the organization, but also the strategies of terrorism are unleashed in accordance with general political directives and agendas."[90]

Even if the community supports this weapon which is legitimized by the religious hierarchy, why are suicide bombings increasing, especially among the young? One explanation is that suicide bombers are seen as successful because their service is for a higher cause;[91] this success "incentivizes those who recruit and send the suicide bombers on their lethal missions."[92] Jessica Stern proposes the answer might be "social contagion:"

> Ordinary suicide has been shown to spread through social contagion especially among youth. Studies have shown that a teenager whose friend or relative commits suicide is more likely to commit suicide himself. Suicide bombing entails a willingness not only to die, but also to kill others. The situation in Gaza suggests that suicide-murder can also be spread through social contagion. "Martyrdom operations" are part of the popular culture. For example, on the streets of Gaza, children play a game call *shuhada,* which includes a mock funeral for a suicide bomber. Teenage rock groups praise martyrs in their songs. Asked to name their heroes, young Palestinians are likely to include suicide bombers.[93]

Research indicates that terrorist organizations will continue to use suicide bomber tactics and employ female suicide bombers. A comprehensive counterterrorism plan should recognize the increasing potential for use of suicide bombers, including females. Specifically, the United States must continue to lead the way in this fight with terrorism. The United States has the capabilities (diplomatic, economic, information, military) to provide leadership in combating these problems.

Diplomatically, the United States should continue to obtain international and United Nations (UN) support in public designation of terrorists, as well as improved information sharing, tightened border security, and reduction of terrorist financing. The UN Security Council adopted Resolution 1373, which requires all states to prevent and suppress the financing of terrorist acts, to include freezing funds and financial assets. In the words of U.S. Secretary of State Colin Powell, "Diplomacy helps us to take the war to the terrorist, to cut off resources they need and depend upon to survive."[94] Reducing their funding and tightening worldwide controls should reduce the global reach of terrorist organizations that employ suicide bombers. Additionally, since the most recent bombings have occurred as a result of the Israeli-Palestinian conflict, the United States needs to push for peaceful resolution of problems in that area.

Worldwide terrorism uses people as bombs under the guise of addressing human problems, so "prevention will require a great improvement in the social conditions that produce, beget, or trigger terrorist acts."[95] Economically, the United States should help develop an "effective counterterrorist strategy that would seek to reduce the terrorist group's base of support through development programs."[96] This aid would provide economic, material, and psychological support to those who have identified with terrorist groups. One major reason Hamas has been so successful is because it provides "social aid" that assists the poor, provides medical care, and educates the children. However, it has also been proven that many of these organizations are merely fronts for funneling money to terrorist organizations. "Fundraising, training, indoctrination, and criminal activities are usually covered by all kinds of harmless organizations ranging from religious to humanitarian institutions."[97] These fronts must be identified, and their funding streams eliminated. At the same time, the true humanitarian need can be met by recognized and authentic relief agencies.

On the information front, several actions are appropriate. First, as noted above, suicide bombers are part of a larger organization. These organizations and their support of suicide terrorists should be made known and roundly castigated by the international community. Their religious rationale should be debunked. They should be condemned widely for attacking noncombatants and for the overwhelming viciousness of their attacks. Suicide bombers should no longer be seen as "victims" but as "assassins." The key is to change peoples' perceptions and thus to deny support for them. Changes in behavior will occur when the community no longer views suicide bombings as accepted, normal—even heroic—behavior. The United States and humanitarian organizations should review the education of younger children in schools that are supported by terrorist organizations, since "pictures of training camps showing small children learning to become suicide bombers have had great impact on public opinion in the international audience."[98] Further, "Goals of a long-range policy should include deterring alienated youth from joining a terrorist organization in the first place. A counterstrategy could be approached within a framework of advertising and civic-action programs which would help to discredit the terrorist group and have a negative impact on their recruitment efforts."[99] For "Without popular support, a terrorist group cannot survive."[100]

The United States should not respond to suicide bombers militarily unless it has specific, credible information that directly links a given organization to terrorists and suicide bombers; however, given that suicide bombers **want** to die, attacking them militarily may only encourage others to take up the cause. Finally, Israel repeatedly has struck against the Palestinians—destroying suicide bombers' homes, displacing their families, militarily retaliating. To date, Israel military responses have engendered an escalating, ever-intensifying hostile reaction. Most importantly, "the question of the moral legitimacy of counterterrorist activities must be analyzed accordingly. How far can a state go in combating terrorism without risking endangering its democratic structure?"[101]

Operationally, the United States must improve its intelligence capability, using both human and technical information gathering. "Intelligence is the first link in the chain of thwarting any terror attack, but is of the utmost importance in thwarting suicide attacks before they are put into practice."[102] In dealing with suicide attacks, the United States should rely on "more and better human intelligence enabling us to penetrate the movement's armies, monitor its recruitment drives, and predict its evolution—including the type of personnel it will recruit."[103] Our counterterrorism strategies should not "rely on standard operation procedures such as race and gender-based profiling,"[104] because doing so "puts the safety of the American people at risk."[105]

Given the globalization of terror from nonstate actors, experts believe that suicide bombings, which will include female suicide bombers, will increase. The next "first" will be the "first" Al Qaeda female suicide bomber. "The Federal Bureau of Investigation has acknowledged that Al Qaeda is actively recruiting women,"[106] perhaps for just this role. International terrorist organizations will assess U.S. security vulnerabilities and exploit weaknesses. While this terrorist weapon may not change the political outcome for the United States or its allies, it will negatively and emotionally impact American lives, beliefs, and morale.

ENDNOTES

1. Don Van Natta, Jr., "Big Bang Theory: The Terror Industry Fields Its Ultimate Weapon," *New York Times,* August 24, 2003, sec. 4, p. 1.

2. Robert A. Pape, "Dying to Kill Us," *New York Times,* September 23, 2003, sec. 1A, p. 19.

3. Yoram Schweitzer, "Suicide Bombings: The Ultimate Weapon?" August 7, 2001; available from *http://www.ict.org.il/ articles/articledet.cfm?articleid=373*; Internet; accessed September 5, 2003.

4. Pape, sec. 1A, p. 19.

5. Department of Homeland Security, *Homeland Security Advisory System Increases to National Level ORANGE,* Alert 03-025, Washington, DC: U.S. Department of Homeland Security, May 20, 2003, p. 2.

6. "Terror Attack Fears," *Sunday Mail (SA),* December 21, 2003, sec. Foreign, p. 35, database on-line; available from Lexis-Nexis; accessed January 15, 2004.

7. Jessica Stern, "When Bombers are Women," *Washington Post,* December 18, 2003, sec. 1A, p. 35.

8. *Ibid.*

9. Clara Beyler, "Messengers of Death, Female Suicide Bombers," February 12, 2003; available from *http://www.ict.org.il/ articles/articledet.cfm?articleid=471*; Internet; accessed September 5, 2003.

10. Ehud Sprinzak, "Rational Fanatics," *Foreign Policy*, September-October 2000, p. 68.

11. Jessica Stern, *Terror in the Name of God,* New York: Harper Collins, 2003, p. xxiii.

12. Amy Waldman, "Masters of Suicide Bombing: Tamil Guerrillas of Sri Lanka," *New York Times,* January 14, 2003, sec. A, p. 1.

13. Boaz Ganor, "The First Iraqi Suicide Bombing. A Hint of Things to Come?" March 30, 2003; available from *http://www.ict.org.il/articles/articledet.cfm?articleid-477*; Internet; accessed September 5, 2003.

14. Cindy C. Combs and Martin Slann, *Encyclopedia of Terrorism*, New York: Facts on File, Inc., 2002, p. 20.

15. Sprinzak, p. 68.

16. Yoram Schweitzer, "Suicide Terrorism: Development & Characteristics," April 21, 2000; available from *http://www.ict.org.il/articles/articledet.dfm?articleid=112*; Internet; accessed September 5, 2003.

17. Ganor, "The First Iraqi Suicide Bombing."

18. Russell D. Howard and Reid L. Sawyer, *Terrorism and Counterterrorism,* Guilford, CT: McGraw-Hill/Dushkin, 2002, p. 130.

19. Stern, *Terror in the Name of God*, p. 40.

20. Arnon Regular, "Mother of Two Becomes First Female Suicide Bomber for Hamas," *Haaretz,* January 16, 2004.

21. *Ibid.*

22. *Ibid.*

23. *Ibid.*

24. Van Natta, sec.4, p. 1.

25. Hala Jaber, "The Avengers," *Sunday Times (London)*, December 7, 2003, sec. Features, p. 1, database on-line; available from Lexis-Nexis; accessed January 15, 2004.

26. *Ibid.*

27. Phillip Smucker, "Arab Women Take to the Streets; Pro-Palestinian Demonstrations in Arab Nations This Week Have Included More Women," *Christian Science Monitor,* April 16, 2002, sec. World, p. 6, database on-line; available from Lexis-Nexis; accessed September 5, 2003.

28. Combs and Slann, p. 215.

29. *Ibid.*, pp. 216-218.

30. *Ibid.*, p. 215.

31. Luisella Neuburger and Tiziana Valentini, *Women and Terrorism*, New York: St. Martin's Press, 1996, p. 24.

32. *Ibid.*

33. Stern, *Terror in the Name of God*, p. 51.

34. Boaz Ganor, "Suicide Terrorism: An Overview," February 15, 2000; available from *http://www.ict.org.il/articles/articl edet.cfm?articleid=128*; Internet; accessed September 5, 2003.

35. Stern, *Terror in the Name of God*.

36. Scott Atran, "Who Wants to be a Martyr?" *New York Times,* May 5, 2003, sec. A, p. 23, database on-line; available from ProQuest; accessed September 16, 2003.

37. Stern, *Terror in the Name of God*.

38. Ganor, "Suicide Terrorism: An Overview."

39. Beyler.

40. "This Litany of Carnage Explodes the Myth That Terrorism Can Be Easily Defeated," *Independent (London),* May 19, 2003, sec. Comment, p. 14, database on-line; available from Lexis Nexis; accessed September 5, 2003.

41. Yoram Schweitzer, "A Fundamental Change in Tactics," *Washington Post,* October 19, 2003, sec. B, p. 3, database on-line; available from Lexis-Nexis; accessed January 15, 2004.

42. Jonathan Kay, "Watching Her Go from a Doll to a Rock to a Bomb," *Los Angeles Times*, January 30, 2002, sec. California Metro, database on-line; available from Lexis-Nexis; accessed September 5, 2003.

43. Randy Boswell, "Black Widows Put Moscow Under Siege: Female Suicide Bombers Spread Wave of Terror Across Russian Capital," *Ottawa Citizen,* July 11, 2003, sec. A, p. 1, database on-line; available from Lexis-Nexis; accessed September 5, 2003.

44. *Ibid.*

45. Mark McDonald, "Chechnya's Eerie Rebels: Black Widows—the 19 Black-Clad Female Terrorists in Moscow's Theater Siege—Are Still Shrouded in Mystery, One Year Later," *Gazette (Montreal, Quebec)*, October 24, 2003, sec. A, p. 4, database on-line; available from Lexis-Nexis; accessed November 7, 2003.

46. Ganor, *Suicide Terrorism: An Overview*.

47. Gregg Zoroya, "Her Decision to be a Suicide Bomber," *USA Today*, April 22, 2003, sec. A, p. 1, database on-line; available from Lexis-Nexis; accessed September 5, 2003.

48. Sprinzak, p. 69.

49. Jeffrey D. Simon, *The Terrorist Trap*, Indianapolis: Indiana University Press, 1994, p. 310.

50. Jaber.

51. Ganor, "Suicide Terrorism: An Overview."

52. Stern, *Terror in the Name of God*.

53. Atran.

54. Yonah Alexander and John M. Gleason, eds., *Behavioral and Quantitative Perspectives on Terrorism*, New York: Pergamon Press, 1981, p. 8.

55. Melanie Reid, "Myth that Women are the Most Deadly Killers of All," *Herald (Glasgow)*, January 29, 2002, sec. A, p. 14, database on-line; available from Lexis-Nexis; accessed September 5, 2003.

56. *Ibid*.

57. Beyler.

58. "The Bomber Next Door," *60 Minutes II*, May 28, 2003, database on-line; available from Lexis-Nexis; accessed September 5, 2003.

59. "Female Suicide Bombers Were Trained Abroad—Russian Security Service," *BBC Worldwide*, database on-line; available from Lexis-Nexis; accessed January 15, 2004.

60. *Ibid*.

61. Argumenty i Fakty, "How Many More Suicide Bombers?" *What the Papers Say (Russia)*, July 11, 2003, sec. Shorts, p. 1, 6, database on-line; available from Lexis-Nexis; accessed January 15, 2004.

62. Luba Vinogradova, "Deadly Secret of the Black Widows," *Times* (London), October 22, 2003, sec. Features, p. 4, database on-line; available from Lexis-Nexis; accessed September 5, 2003.

63. Matthew Kalman, "Inside the Mind of a Suicide Bomber; Recruit Reveals Training of Females for Mission," *Standard* (St. Catharines), May 31, 2002, sec. C, p. 10, database on-line; available from Lexis-Nexis; accessed September 5, 2003.

64. Jaber.

65. Margo Harakas, "Palestinian Women Defy Islamic Tradition to Become Suicide Bombers," *Sun-Sentinel*, April 15, 2002, sec. Lifestyle, p. 10, database on-line; available from Lexis-Nexis; accessed September 5, 2003.

66. Howard and Sawyer, p. 129.

67. "This Litany of Carnage."

68. Schweitzer.

69. Howard and Sawyer, p. 130.

70. Stern, *Terror in the Name of God*, p. 52.

71. Jonathan Kay, "Defaming Islam—One Bomb at a Time," *National Post* (Canada), July 16, 2003, sec. A, p. 14, database on-line; available from Lexis-Nexis; accessed September 5, 2003.

72. Howard and Sawyer.

73. Stern, *Terror in the Name of God*.

74. Beyler.

75. "Lebanese Muslim Cleric OK's Female Suicide Bombers," *Business Recorder*, April 2, 2002, database on-line; available from Lexis-Nexis; accessed September 5, 2003.

76. Harakas.

77. Howard and Sawyer, p. 128.

78. Schweitzer.

79. "Bin Laden Sets up Female Suicide Squads to Bomb U.S.," *Agence France Presse*, March 12, 2003, sec. International News, database on-line; available from Lexis-Nexis; accessed September 5, 2003.

80. *Ibid.*

81. Schweitzer.

82. Sprinzak, p. 69.

83. Stern, *Terror in the Name of God*, p. 51.

84. Sprinzak.

85. *Ibid.*, p. 72.

86. *Ibid.*, p. 69.

87. Van Natta.

88. Combs and Slann, p. 84.

89. Atran.

90. Howard and Sawyer, p. 128.

91. Combs and Slann, p. 213.

92. Alan M. Dershowitz, *Why Terrorism Works*, New Haven, CT: Yale University Press, 2002, p. 26.

93. Stern, *Terror in the Name of God*, pp. 52-53.

94. Congress, House, International Relations Committee, *Hearing of the International Terrorism, Nonproliferation, and Human Rights Subcommittee of the House International Relations Committee*, March 26, 2003.

95. Yonah Alexander and John M. Gleason, eds., *Behavioral and Quantitative Perspectives on Terrorism*, New York: Pergamon Press, 1981, p. 30.

96. Rex A. Hudson, "The Sociology and Psychology of Terrorism: Who Becomes a Terrorist and Why?" *Library of Congress,* September, 1999, database on-line; available from Lexis-Nexis; accessed September 5, 2003.

97. Eric Herren, "Counter-Terrorism Dilemmas," April 15, 2002; available from *http://222.ict.org.il/articles/articledet.cfm?articleid=432*; Internet; accessed September 5, 2003.

98. *Ibid.*

99. Hudson.

100. *Ibid.*

101. Herren.

102. Ganor, "Suicide Terrorism: An Overview."

103. Stern, "When Bombers are Women."

104. *Ibid.*

105. *Ibid.*

106. *Ibid.*

www.ingramcontent.com/pod-product-compliance
Lightning Source LLC
Chambersburg PA
CBHW081144280526
45787CB00007B/3215